What We Can See

By Chera Van Falcon Burg

What We Can See

Poems

Chera Van Falcon Burg

Four
Windows
Press

Four Windows Press

Sturgeon Bay, WI 54235

Fourwindowspress1@gmail.com

Chera Van Falcon Burg, 2024
www.cheravanfalconburg.com

Publisher's Note: This is a work of poetry. Names, characters, places, and incidents are a product of the author's imagination. Locales and public names are sometimes used for atmospheric purposes. Any resemblance to actual people, living or dead, or to businesses, companies, events, institutions, or locales is completely coincidental.

Book Layout © 2017 BookDesignTemplates.com

What We Can See, Chera Van Falcon Burg -- 1st ed.

Cover Photo by Chera Van Falcon Burg
Author Photo by Karen Burns

ISBN 979-8-9905946-0-9

Dedication

To the natural world and the wisdom of the wild. May it infuse us with knowing and make us wiser.

Acknowledgments

I am grateful to the editors of the following publications in which my poems previously appeared:

Eco-Theo Review: Out of Thin Air
Canary – A Literary Journal of the Environmental Crisis: What We
    Know
Hal Prize Finalist, 2022: Where The House Had Been
Wisconsin Poets' Calendar: Last Rose
Moss Piglet: Song of Earth (I Contain Multitudes)
Peninsula Pulse: This Morning and What Came Before
Newport State Park Poetry Trail: What Was and What We Know

I am thankful to Writers & Books in Rochester, New York for their offering of poetry classes over the years and to Charles Coté for a year of poetry classes there. I am grateful to the National Poetry Week celebrations in San Francisco, California and the San Francisco Bay Area poets who helped shape my poetry. I am grateful to musician, Hans Christian, for our poetry and music performances in the US, Mexico, and Europe. I am thankful to Write On Door County in Fish Creek, Wisconsin for creating a vibrant poetry community and to Nan Cohen for her invaluable poetry Master Class at Write On.

I am particularly grateful to Estella Lauter for introducing me to the poets of Door County, Wisconsin and securing my place in three poetry groups there. I am also grateful to my fellow poets in those groups whose work inspires me. I am indebted to Estella Lauter, Ralph Murre, Thomas Davis and Ethel Mortenson Davis for their meaningful critiques of the manuscript for this book. Finally, I am grateful to my brother, Eric Van Valkenburg, for so willingly listening to earlier versions of my poems with his writerly ear.

CONTENTS

First Roots: The Life We Are Given

Roots in Nature: The Life We Find

Re-conceiving and Re-imagining: What We Can See

What We Can See

First Roots:

The Life We Are Given

Alchemy

The time between the child
and the girl she becomes
is a dance of fire lit from within.

The distance between the girl
and the home she leaves
is a calculation of roots and stars.

The journey of the woman
and the mysteries she finds
is the alchemy of seeing beyond.

Beyond Prayer

I placed the injured in grass-lined shoeboxes,
young birds and rabbits, my child eyes
watching over their helplessness

as I prayed to the only god I knew, though
his miracles were unreliable. Still, I pushed
against his great gray shape and hoped

he would be moved enough to crack open
an eye. Muted by a father's violence, a child
is drawn to tend the voiceless

and learns to look beyond the god she is given
to find her own sanctuary. I was safest outside
my father's house, past the threshold

of his impulses, where I followed birds nested
beneath the cover of canopy, watched deer
gather fawns as they disappeared

into dusk, rose at dawn to see the red fox weave
her kits phantom-like through blackberry
brambles. It was the wild that taught me

of family, where I witnessed love and devotion,
saw their natural instinct to protect the young,
to nurture innocence, unlike

the inclinations of my father. In the primal air
of nature, undiluted by human beliefs, faith
was free of the need for prayer

or persuasion to invoke miracles. Here, miracles
were as reliable as the glisten of dew on blades
of grass beneath the muted blue hues

of a morning sky, constant as songbirds opening
the day, innate as a child's love of the world
far from an idle, heavy-lidded god.

Fire and Water

Built a century ago on stolen land, the house was already
tear-stained when we moved in decades later. The year

after it was built, two hundred acres surrounding the house
became the first county park – a small plaque the only telling

it was ancestral land of the Onöndowa'ga where the ground
is salted with sorrow and songs of return waft in the air.

When we bought the old house, we didn't listen to its talk
of not belonging on the land where rains came every spring,

spilling over creekbanks, flooding meadows and woodlands,
leaving only a small island around the house. Our father

tried to pump the water out as it climbed pitted cellar walls,
while our mother prayed for the rain to stop as if it was

the fault of water that the house sat on a flood plain. We,
the six children growing here, worshipped the water,

its presence able to transform our dry, dissonant world
into an aquatic sanctuary of golden carp and singing frogs,

emerald-headed ducks and tuxedoed geese enchanting
us with wildness. It was the way of water that saved us,

carried us beyond the boundaries of a broken family fixed
between walls holding stains and tears of a hundred years.

Decades later, our father gone, the children now grown,
mother alone, the park bought the house for the land,

set it on fire for practice, doused it down to ash, unaware
the union of fire and water would ignite a restoration.

Where The House Had Been

As I stood where the house had been, the morning fog
licked at my feet like our old black dog and cloaked

my body in a dream-like mist of the past where I saw
the walls of the house burning and the roof collapse

with an upward whoosh of air feeding the steeple
of flames until a blessing of ash blackened the earth.

As the fog thinned, I saw the old oaks and willows
still here, standing like ancestors marking the place

where the house was missing, water pooled in circles
round their roots in the flooded meadow as shadows

of water birds glided between. It was here the child
I was had grown, her small body bent from sorrow

sowed in this place, carried as an ache through my life,
though the light in her eyes still rises in mine.

When the fog burned away, what had been held within
the troubled house lifted with the smoke, becoming sky,

its story no longer lodged in my body, but returned
to the land where it belonged, where it would speak

of the four directions, the turn of seasons, of earth
and sky, fire and water, and the fresh, fertile ash.

The Weight of Being

1.

We followed our father's restless wanderings,
mandatory disciples like our mother, pinned
as she was in the bondage of an early marriage
and young children. All of us huddled
like minnows under his shadow, scooped up
one day in his latest impulse, emptied out
into a railcar on a westbound train,
its departing whistle sounding like a dirge.
The clack of crossties in rhythm
with our trepidation as we waited for derailment
of a man driven by ruins of a childhood
cobbled into a self as fragile as his history.

2.

We fell rapt in his tales, etched with the magic
a child finds even in the dire, like the story
he told of being sent to live with his widowed,
Scottish grandmother when he was only two
after his mother died in childbirth
leaving five more behind to be farmed out
to relatives. Each time he told the story
he was carried back to his grandmother's farm
where he slept in her soft arms every night
as they waited for the ghost of his grandfather
to appear at the footboard. He told of the way
they whispered of their love for each other
and for him, the small boy in their keep.
He saw the pull of death as his grandfather
disappeared into the light of morning
and felt the depth of their long promise

19

to be together again when they would rise
like mist over hills and sea in the old country.

3.

Two years later, the boy left his grandmother's
house when his father found a new immigrant wife
and took the children back to the home
where the black and white photo of their mother
watched over them, out of sight, high up
on a kitchen shelf, the same photo that looked
over us from the black marble top table
in our living room, her face forever locked
in a wistful look as if she knew her fate,
her small ghostly fingers braided beneath
her chin like an Irish knot, the deep pools
of her eyes taking in the childhood stories
our father told over and over, as if the telling
could bring back a simpler time when a boy
could find adventure in gathering tin cans
he sold for pennies to survive during
the Great Depression, or of waking up under
snow covered blankets in a broken-down house,
five siblings curled together in one bed
to stay warm, as close as they ever would be.

4.

When he told of scrapes with kid street gangs
and escapes from his father's belt or the blade
of a bread knife his step-grandmother
shook at him as she cursed him in Italian,
he would laugh until his body shook and tears
streaked his face. It was then that we loved him,
bonded over generations of trauma, the long
genealogy of brokenness. What other life
could he live but one desperate to fill

the emptiness of a boy left alone to find ways
to matter, to be bigger than what was lost?
We were the cloth, the loft and fill, stitched
too tightly, the thread to make him feel whole.

5.

When our train reached California, he forged
a frenzied trail up the coast, eight of us
in a rented Econoline, our breathing rapid
with fear and excitement in the clutch
of a man driving too fast as if to outrun
the press of the past until the blue
of the ocean stopped him, lulled him in
with the pull of its waves like a mother's arms,
the warm sand like a cradle for the lost
and driftless, blanketed with ice poppies
the color of love. Further north, drawn by
the benevolent gaze of coastal redwoods,
he gathered us beneath their towering canopy,
into light-stained cathedral groves where
we fell on soft red ground of fallen needles,
the only time we were a family at peace.

6.

Too soon we were back on the road where
he drove too close to the steep edge
of the winding Pacific Coast Highway,
as if he would go over – his way to be a man
in charge of his destiny and ours.
His delight at our chorus of screams
was enough to divert him, to give him back
a sense of control, enough to be done
with the golden lure of the west.
He loaded us like chattel onto the next
eastbound train, our fate looking up
as we headed toward home to the place
where our fragile hope was kept.

Camped in domes of passenger cars,
we wound through dark tunnels in broken
mountains as we watched the west dissolve
into the grasslands of plains and prairies.

7.

We rode tracks through Midwest farmlands
all night as fields of corn became endless
dark blue waves until the light of dawn
when we crossed the Mississippi,
headed toward Chicago. As we got closer
to the Great Lake of home our small, vigilant
bodies eased slightly like young rabbits
when they sense danger has passed for now.
Our natural instincts grew stronger the nearer
we came to the safety we knew in the wild
places of our birth – under the cover
of tall grasses in northeast meadows, high
in the arms of red oaks where we hung
like prayer flags, hidden in sunlit temples
of white pine, or following the flow of water
as it guided our flimsy canoe through
creek bends and tall cat-tailed wetlands
all the way to Lake Ontario with its expanse
of possibility. Like all other creatures,
we knew it was nature that saved us,
from California to our New York home,
its insistence infused in our tissue,
thickened into new skin of childhood resilience.

8.

One by one we aged out of captivity, while
our father aged into melancholy, his kingdom
crumbled into ruin, the intense blue of his eyes
faded into the reprieve of an early death.
Captive now only to our strange inheritance
of inexplicable longings and brief bouts

of madness, the ones that suddenly arise
when the soul is desperate to find its place
along some elusive, redemptive edge,
a momentary release from the weight
of being, the place our father could not find.

Refrain

I followed the salty taste of my longings like a river intent
on emptying out into the open sea.

Left behind: The wreck of an early marriage, shards
of another love, and the small, abandoned children of my sister.

In my absence: A death, the family home demolished
clean, the children disappeared into their own restlessness.

Decades gone, an unexpected instinct cast a return like a bird
seeking self-remnants, the nest of remains.

Still here: A last parent, roots of siblings grown deep
in home ground, traces of a life no longer mine.

On the land where the house once stood, the late afternoon sun
tinted the sky indigo as a vast flock of geese flew low overhead,

their black and white set in deepening blue, their refrain as loud
and clear as I have ever heard, taking a lifetime to pass over me.

The Life We Find

This morning
in the thin space
between dream
and waking,
layers of my life
dropped away
from the frame
of my body –

the thick shrouds
of a father's need
to make me feel
small
so he could be
more
than a broken man,

the dark wounds
inflicted
by a lover's anger,
the kind
that broke me,
made me feel
like nobody
because he needed
someone
to blame for what
he was not.

When a dream
guides us,
we begin to molt
the feathers
and fur

that our animal
instincts
have grown
as a cover
for all the times
we were told
to hide
who we were.

Underneath
we find
new growth,
light as air,
decades late
but not too late
to let go
of the life
we were given
and keep
the one we find.

Roots in Nature:

The Life We Find

Return

I came back to the ocean, the one
my father's westward longings
reached decades ago, igniting
my own. I returned to release
a childhood into the boundless
Pacific where its blue trance
of waves rise and fall
as the pull of water smooths over
old tracks etched in shifting
sand, erasing what was, offering
the blank slate of what might be.

I miss the places I once called home
and yearn for places I have yet
to find, drawn as I am to follow
a call that by its clutch
feels ancestral, as if ancient
sea cliffs and far northern fjords
were carved into the geography
of my body, shaping me
to wander as I seek some truth

or knowing as quiet and fleeting
as late afternoon sunlight
sifting through trees in thin,
slanted rails lighting my face
with wonder before it slips
into darkness, leaving me alone
to ponder where I am going,
not knowing if I will arrive.

When I drift too far, I come back
to where I began, to the place
of a Great Lake's waters

29

What We Can See

and the meadow's marshy edge
where I find the wild roses
wilted and fallen, the ones
I've grieved for years, where
I find comfort in the constancy
of ruin, in the way it holds
the essence, the perfect
trace of each petal's return.

What We Know

My days are measured by light,
not time. No longer living
a life of rootless velocity

and mad harvesting, I am
a fallow field unfettered
by purpose except to find

those moments that stop
my breath with quiet beauty
barely sensed without

Walden-like stillness. My pond
is a neighborhood in winter
where I, the visitor,

wander empty streets between
shuttered houses sheltered in
solitude. Drifting over

wordless white fields, I sense
the dormant waiting beneath,
rooted in the wisdom

of darkness, trusting in death
and rebirth, knowing the soft
shoots of new life will

once again find the light. I trust
in this place, deeply listening
to the fervent bird

sing out its solitary song
knowing darkness will return
the light, and life reflect it.

Brief Presence

Mornings are for watching,
for looking out over the horizon
as if the body is at sea
or atop a fire tower, wired as it is
to scan for signs of danger.
Stationed at my kitchen window,
I watch over this bayside hill
though dangers here happen slowly,
the kind we won't notice in time,
like the missing we don't count
until far too many have gone.

I don't watch from fear, I watch
from longing for what still lingers
at the edge of awareness,
a pale presence of what was lost
in the shaping of a child
or a culture, to cut the wild out,
not knowing how dangerous
we would become and how alone.

I watch for signs of a way back
to the wild, back to knowing
how to live an Earthly life
with all other beings
bound together – a brief presence
in the vast sweep of a universe.

This Morning

This morning a blaze of color broke through
my windowed gaze, orange flare so bright

it lit the dull green spines of aloe growing tight
and twisted as blackberries, its quick flits

like tiny bursts of fireworks waking the purple
soaked spikes of Pride of Madeira that grope

the upward slope. Still for a moment, it shaped
into Oriole, its name from old French or Latin,

meaning *golden*. This one called Hooded, the first
one seen in the rounded ravine surrounding

the worn-out cottage I called home those last
years in California, years turned inward,

senses shuttered against the slow burgeoning
of an ungentle culture bent on oblivion

in a climate of drought and fire. Saturated in
aliveness of luminous bird, I sprung open

like a rusted lock on an old trunk holding a life,
its tattered straps snapping free. As I stumbled

out, untethered into the light, bare feet following
eyes tracking beloved bird, I bowed down

to its nature, the curve of my body knowing it is
my nature, the way to move through this world.

Unspoken Conversation

Bird and woman,
an age-old dyad.
Their gaze a language
without words,
an unspoken conversation
held in the curve
of a wing,
the bend of a limb,
an unbroken bond
that cannot be erased.

Imprint

We leave our marks on this life,
sometimes gently, sometimes not,
some leave scars, others
disappear and some shed light.

Our lives leave traces set in stone
like fossils of wings or bones,
while others crumble with years
like the small handprint cast
in the clay of childhood,
fingers misshapen in the drying,
foretelling the way a body
will slip its boundaries over time.

When we leave our imprint of ash
or bone like a late autumn leaf
as it falls with all the others
onto damp ground, it will be
one last mark, a testament
to the inexplicable beauty
and terror that is this Earthly life.

Space of A Tree

Jags of lightning shoot
like crooked arrows
from sky to earth,
trailed by thunder's ascent
from rumble to roar.
Rain heavy as boulders
all night, bent on havoc.

Paradise apple still standing,
each leaf cupping water
like small shields
over bright green fruit,
too small to feed the hungry.

At dawn, battered branches
draped too low to the ground,
old roots no longer able
to tread water-logged earth
finally let go, cracking the air
loud as a siren, sounding
the call to the young,
an offering of sacred space.

Field of Time

Waves of snow drift from field to forest edge, motionless
except for swirls the wind stirs over the surface,

white except for tints of blue and gray, hints of opaline
in the bright glisten of late afternoon sunlight.

Things are not what they seem, I whisper. Look deeper,
I tell my eyes. What is beneath I ask, knowing

we carry vestiges of evolution as we form in our mother's
body – the genetic code of our bodies like a collective

memory. As I stand as one relative with my feet planted
in this winter field, I feel the presence of ancestors

in this moment that required all of time to arrive. Here,
between field and forest is the portal to all moments

that evolved in this place – a collage of the multitudes
of animal journeys laid in patterns, prints and tracks,

connected by scent and touch as they traverse human
intersections and intervals of time – layered with cycles

of seasons where buds unfold into leaves and blossoms
to become the first signs of spring as bulbs break open

old ground and erupt into the color of wildflower flocks
while green shoots of young grass emerge, growing tall

before they burn into the amber of late summer, foretelling
the time when leaves will turn red, orange and yellow,

the brilliant paint of fall, falling with silver frost, returning
to shades of white that will once again cover this field of time.

Another Way

In midwinter, a migrant from western
wildfires in a time when glaciers
are melting faster than we thought,
a time when our way of living
in the world is dangerous and broken,

I think of the wild blue irises, the way
they rise up and break abruptly
into spring, eager to be of Earth again.

When the ground is frozen, I find them
only on the page, diagrammed and labeled
into parts, flattened into a way of knowing
where their essence is missing—

    The vivid beauty
of violet blue existing
to enter an eye

    The curled shape
of petals holding a teardrop
of luminous yellow

    The silent signal
of complementary colors
heard by pollinators

    The swoon
of nectar on the tongue
of hummingbirds

    The awe of art
so freely offered to all
who pass by.

What We Can See

In midwinter, I am reminded
there are those things
worth waiting for, whether
it takes a year or a lifetime.

There are those among us
whose essence breaks through
what flattens our own
and shows us another way.

Song of Earth

~ a riff on Walt Whitman's *Song of Myself, 51*

I sing to myself when I am alone, soft notes in winter
for what has passed, louder in spring for what will be,
in harmony with what I am when summer comes.

I tell of my past in rock and stone, promising nothing
but to spin in time around the sun with seven more
at home in an ancient sky as we sing our old refrain.

I watch the moon hum herself into fullness as nights
of stars come and go, while the tides sing their part
in ebbs and flows in tune with the ocean's undertow.

I feel the sun unfold the night into the light of a new day
as he reminds us to sing before it's too late, make up
the words as we go, the chorus we already know.

(I am large, I contain multitudes.)

Rootless:

Disconnection with Nature

What Came Before

What came before the crush of houses built dense
as corn rows thinning the air, before the land

was flattened and dulled into squares, patched with
stray grass, leaving tracks of annihilation?

Glacier-carved ridges were here with dense bones
of dolostone, muscled in layers of sandstone,

shale and limestone that descended into the tissue
of valleys tarped with the textured skin of soil,

veined with water circulating with air and sunlight,
seeding the centuries with red oak, sugar maple,

white pine, beech, birch, eastern cedar and hemlock
as they rooted into networks, co-evolved with fungi

and other kin to become webbed into a forest, its hum
felt in the fringe of wild-flowered meadows as they

stretched to the edge of cat-tail marshes that bowed
to riparian sycamores and willows as they wept

of their love for water cradled in bending creekbanks
as it flowed to release into the Great Lake, the one

called Niigaani-gichigami – leading sea or Oniataríːio,
lake of shining waters, by the first ones here.

What Was

What becomes of the soul of a place
when its land is taken, its waters
exiled, the wild erased?

An Elder once said the displaced spirit
goes into the heart of the mountain
and waits for harmony

to return to the land. When the soul
of a place is missing, what becomes
of a child raised there?

When forests are felled, whole families
of trees, even ones with nests holding
small, speckled eggs

incubating life, what becomes of wonder?
What was here was home to all beings
who wandered the wild air,

they were relations of place, woven into
the mystery, not of being *on* the Earth,
but being *of* the Earth.

If you had been a child here, the call
of wild geese would inhabit your own
crying out. It might explain

your migratory ways and why you keep
trying to find your way back home,
back to what was

At the Edge

Standing atop the Northern Salinian Block where it rises
above the slide of the San Andres Fault,

I wonder if it was the gods who arranged the terrain here,
flipping tectonic plates perhaps for pleasure

some 20 million years ago. Who else could move granite
like it was a lump of clay, where it would watch

over the endless Pacific abyss, where the blue hues of sea
and sky merge, melting the horizon as if the veil

between worlds had lifted? Here a body at the brink is drawn
to cast into the ancient and formless,

into the bliss of being no longer separate, not alone, not other
but a rising wave or a ray of light.

From here you would never know what we have done, how
we have nearly suckled the life from our mother

for our pleasure, like little gods gulping for more even as we
gasp for breath. When she takes her last breath,

and our round, naked bodies beach on her dry breasts,
we will know we were never gods.

Aftermath

When finally we stop,
consumed by the violence
of our needs,
when we stare out and see
with the burned eyes
of mortality,
we will be stunned
quiet and fall
into the earth's soft
blackness, into
the aftermath,
the sealed lips of God
or Gaia – or love.

All That Remains

As the light of Earth wanes,
will we finally gather
what we've neglected
and sift through
our scattered intentions
as they swirl around us
like last leaves letting go?

Will we keep what feels true
and find in our heart
what once was home, where
we were never separate
from Rock, Tree, Sky or Water?

In the loom of a lost future,
will we turn inward
to mend what has broken
and tend to our bonds,
human and beyond?

As dusk rises, will we seek
our way back like birds
or other wanderers
looking for what was left
untended, whether
Nest, Den, Stream or Soul?

When we return in darkness,
late with our frail hope
to bring back what was lost,
to undo what we've done,
will the threads of our bodies
feel the pull of unraveling?

What We Can See

Will we pray for one last chance
to come together as one
before all that remains
is a sweet, Earthly scent
wafting the thin air
where our home once was?

Activist Turned Lover

I turned my hope
into love,
found love in anger
and despair,
became a lover shouting
of my love
for the singing
that still comes at dawn,
for the water
still falling over bedrock,
for the trees
still standing beneath
the open sky
as it watches over
what is left.

I love what exists
no longer and all
that remains
even as we continue
to extinguish it.

Love is the only action
left to take
and if it's too late,
it will be love
that is left
to fill the infinite hole
in our Earthly heart.

Cooldown

When the Earth moves on,
long tired of us,
weary of rising temperatures,
the endless burning

and melting, she will open
her glacial gates
and let the blue cooldown
her scarred skin.

As she becomes water
once again, she will wash over
all of us and dissolve
our small bodies
back to the beginning.

In time, she will expand
with her galaxy and dance
toward distant stars,
almost as if we never were.

In the Wake of Man

News Headlines 2023:
Canada had its worst wildfire season ever recorded. Smoke from
Canadian forest fires drifted thousands of miles causing poor air
quality across North America and Europe. Unprecedented
European wildfires caused devastating environmental damage and loss
of life. Four simultaneous heat domes caused record heat waves
around the world. This year smashed the record for the world's
hottest by a huge margin. The Earth's oceans had the hottest
temperatures ever recorded. Ten countries in twelve days were hit
with severe flooding. Drought caused reduced crop yields and
raised food prices world-wide. UN report says the world is headed
towards environmental tipping points that are likely to cause
irreversible damage to water supplies and other life-sustaining
systems.

Smoke has no regard
for the boundaries of men
heat and fire the same.

Floods have no concern
for roads and structures of man
rain falls where it will.

When water is gone
climate denial won't quench
the thirst of a child.

In the human age
what is left of the future
in the wake of man?

No Difference – Three Haiku

1.

Your story or mine
their history, his or hers
will be told as one.

2.

What we hold or not
whether embraced or shunned
will still break the heart.

3.

When birds sing at dawn
when we do not know our song
nature hears them both.

Stranger Who May Not Be Born

> I write poems for a stranger who will be born in some
> distant country hundreds of years from now. – *Mary Oliver*

Hundreds of years from now in our human wake,
the livable Earth will likely be long gone
and our books will have been swallowed

by rising seas, their pages perfectly decomposed
on ocean floors with the watery mounds
of our bodies – or the cloth of their spines

will have been parched in the unlivable heat,
crumbled to ash next to small, round piles
of our bones turned the rust of desert dust.

Stranger, who may not be born, I cannot write
for you; I cannot tell you I am sorry we took
your future. But I can promise not to make

wild prophetic claims of posterity or declare
with the danger of empty hope that I write poems
as if there will be a world hundreds of years
from now with anyone left to read them.

But what I can do is write of now – of this one
precious life on this one precious Earth
and fight with words of love as my weapon,
with a mother's energy in my pen to protect

a future that was never mine to squander, not
so you can read my small poems, but so you
might someday be born on a still verdant
Earth and love it too as you write your own.

Uprooted:

Grief And Transcendence

Out of Thin Air

Signs come out of nowhere
like the small dark bird that fell
from the night sky onto the gray

stoop of my mother's grieving
house, the heart-shaped fold of
its wings illuminated in the soft

porch light. Mourning husband,
father, grandfather, we gathered
around the mysterious shape,

holding its presence, circling
the tangle of feelings hardened
between us, unable to find

words through the language of
grief. Keeping vigil, we heard
its name sung out of thin air.

Catbird. Slowly, we began
to mimic each other's voices,
not with words, but with song.

The Other Side

When he tipped a glass of spirits,
he drank the ancient voice,
each sip a lilt rising, a song
in time and place. His face became
his grandfather's face, years
falling to rock and spray
as the green and mist grew
in his eyes like a dance of sea light
and cloud shadow reflected
in their blue. He sang notes
of lyrical laughter with brooding
undertones, full of life
but with an eye on the grave.

When he made the final crossing,
it was a coming home.
Though born with an ocean
between, the Isle was in him,
in every ancestral cell.
For that is the way of separation,
where else can sorrow go,
but into the blood, into the swell
of ancestors long gone
and generations yet to come?

This is why we pray and wait
for visions, why we turn
the soil and watch for signs.
It is why we seek our voice
in the dark sea of night;
it is how we know the other side.

Begin Again

I center my body on a blue mat
like a dot circled in red on a cosmic map,
eyes closed to the world as I watch
my thoughts and empty the dark
corners of my mind. But what of shelter

found in darkness, where grief and love
linger, where memories of loss
seek comfort from the glare of living,
where light waits in the wings
for as long as it takes to be invited in?

Begin Again.

No need to separate self from mind.
Be the trail of thoughts that come
and go like clouds or waves
or the shimmer of stars that appear
in the dark folds of a night sky.

Watch the play of light and shadow,
see how they exist within the other.
Look at the way the trees
are not separate from the constant
chatter of their infinite leaves.

Illuminations of Grief

I gather the falling petals
of grief into upward
turned palms and release
their soft skins
into the widening circle
of sorrow until only
the silent stalk remains.

Fallen lilies and irises wait
in dark earth to bud
and become again. Plucked
from this earth, where
do our loved ones wait?

Pressed against the solidness
of death, I grow afraid
my eyes will forget the fix
of your gaze, empty arms
will no longer feel the swell
of our embrace, fingertips
will become numb to the soft
knowing of your touch.

I grasp memories of you
as they rise like fluff
from winter milkweed
carried with the light
to a vanishing point,
leaving a faint sense
of you, like a fragrance
hints of its essence
but is not, is not you.

What We Can See

In the fullness of absence,
grief circles my body
like rings of a tree,
embedding each fiber
of our history – the life
we once knew, now
a way to be close to you.

Grief's constancy guides
the lone transformation
into the new self
I must now be, rising
not from loss, but from
love returning
like the moon, invisible
in daylight, becoming
brilliantly illuminated
in the bloom of darkness.

Morning Blessing

As I stood in line behind you
cradling my morning newspaper,
I watched the rosary spiral

through the thick of your fingers,
the thread to what once mattered.
Your face was a shade

of scarlet, like a star-cut jewel set
in the faded age of your blue suit,
the cloth that had worn

the decades with you. There was
something in the way your back
fell rounded, shoulders bent

like wings shielding the dark
mystery of your heart, the hint
you had reached the grail

too soon. As you turned to leave,
your eyes flashed back and locked
with mine as if you had seen

some distant watcher – like God.
In that moment, there flickered
a slight lift of your spirit

like you'd been given a sign.
When you crossed the threshold,
the neck of a bottle clasped

gently in your hand like the stem
of a rose, I did the only thing
I could; I blessed the holy wine.

Blank Page

The
old
poet
watches clouds
rise on the blank page
waits for new rain to fill her eyes.

Call Out

When the body is alone too long, it fades
from separation, and the absence of touch
alters the sense of being solid. That is when

I wrap mine in wool, take it to woods or water,
find birds for company, tell it the presence
of nature is enough. When we go back

home, I feed it what it loves, pour wine, play
music, read poetry, talk of how we love
solitude and the connection to something

deeper it brings, explain again that alone is not
the same as lonely. It is soothed for a while,
but the body knows isolation is not solitude,

it knows it comes from a tribe, is meant to be
a social animal, and sooner or later loneliness
will break it. The mind too will become tired,

weary of the rattle of its own thoughts, alone
with the long echo of grief for what's been lost,
for what is missing. When we are alone

too long, we fall into the place between being
and not being like the last breath as it leaves
the pale lips of those we love, those we miss.

When a Canada Goose loses its mate, it waits
alone, calling out a loud and insistent note
that reverberates over the lake, alerting

What We Can See

the V-shaped procession overhead, until pairs
drop down, skidding into a watery landing,
their voices raised in a blaring chorus

as they circle their lone kin, seeming to know
that proximity shows that grief belongs not
to one, but to all. The grieving goose will stay

alone to tend its sorrow as the others fly off
and will wait in solitude until it is time to find
another mate. But if it does not, it will still

rejoin the flock, help raise the young of others,
though it may continue to call out and wait
for its loved one's return. But unlike us,

in our modern epidemic of loneliness, the goose
does not have to wait alone, and unlike too many
of us, it knows its tribe and place in the world.

In the night, there are times I feel the presence
of those who have gone and those I never found
like the air of another world and I call out.

Last Rose

When I become the rose
of late summer – more petals
fallen than remain –
my story will no longer be
words or decades
of memories, but silken
shards scattered
like bright, new seeds
carried to an open horizon
of unimaginable
colors and infinite,
inconceivable patterns.

The River to the Forever Sea

~ inspired by Thomas Davis's poem,
IN MEMORIAM: And Now Joe McDonald

In this place of rivers, earth and sea
we are bound by a body
bound by time, inside a mind
that imagines beyond
and longs for times gone by
as it hopes for brighter times
to be, as though time
could be rearranged or changed,
taken back or set ahead.

But time is bound to become
the years of a life gathered
into the meaning we have tried
to make inside the time
we are here in this world
where love is paired
with grief and loss, though
we would love all over again.

Who can say why we are here
or where we go when time
runs out, but there are some
who can hear the sacred
river's roar, who glimpse
the ones that time let go
dancing in the cataract mist,
their spirits no longer bound,
those who are free to flow
with the river to the forever sea.

When All We Want

What do we do when we witness suffering
so great we are wrapped in its grief,
when all we want to do is be a shield
against violence and hatred,
when there is no one side we can take
that is without blame?

Where do we stand when we want to be
at the side of the injured and innocent,
when we want to dig the living out
of the rubble and wipe
the blood from every child's face?

What do we do when all we want is not war
but peace and justice for all beings,
when all we want to do is explode
with love and infiltrate
the hearts and minds of every human

being on this earth until there is a cease fire
into a new way that has nothing to do
with war or winning, a way so disarming
we come undone and remake the world?

When we no longer want to be possessed
by words or acts of inequality,
what new vision will arise, what new
Great Law of Peace* will we conceive?

*The Great Law of Peace was the founding constitution of the Six Nations
Iroquois Confederacy (Mohawk, Onondaga, Oneida, Cayuga, Seneca &
Tuscarora), which the first five nations ratified in 1450, and added the sixth
nation, the Tuscarora, in 1722. The principles were peace, equity and justice, and
unity.

Re-conceiving and Re-imagining:

What We Can See

Breathe In This Life

I long for a language without words
like proof or truth that does not speak
of faith or belief,

a language free of concepts that blur
the mystery of who we are, who
all beings are.

I want to hear the language carried
in the dust of stars, formed from
cosmic sounds

heard in the pops and vibrations
whispered by trees through threads
of fungi that speak

in sparks root to root as they hum
the forest into an orchestra streaming
notes of wood and fiber

tuned to the flow of water and wing
beats of bees as the rhythm of our
body keeps time,

leaving space for silence between
notes as we listen and breathe in
the nature of this life.

Winged Ancestors

I remember entering this world
breaking through membrane
and mineral, under the warm
cloak of my mother's wings,
high in the arms of home,
the green of its foliage
filtering sunlight too bright
for new, unopened eyes.

There were others crowding
the circle of twigs and down,
our heavy-headed bodies
pushed to the edge. I was the one
to fall, descending to earth
with pin feather wings not ready
to fly, tiny tucked feet unable
to stand. My small body mutated
midair – grew legs to break
my fall, sprouted arms
to touch the hard ground.

When they found me, slumped
at the base of a great tree,
my senses askew, they said
I was theirs, claimed
they had birthed me, though
I never believed them.

As I grew, I kept flapping
my long, bony arms,
tried to hop on stilt-like legs,
preened my soft, downy
hair into a feathered crown.

What We Can See

When they called me daughter,
I sang loudly over their chatter,
wildly chirped the songs
of my winged ancestors
asking to be lifted up, up, up.

We Alone Are Trees

We are not your bent and broken,
you who break the world.
We are not your anthropomorphized,
non-human kin.

We are healers here, unlike you
and most of your kind,
though there are some among you
who are in our keep,
those of you who weep with us,
who once were trees.

China Bird

I come to you
as a small, winged object
not for flight
but for remembering
what it is to shape desire
into beauty,
to feel the curve
of nature,
the instinct of song.

Dark Blue Night

~ inspired by Ethel Mortenson Davis's pastel with poem titled
The Moon

Blue moon of a dark night
caught me,
not by the throat as it did
the artist,
but by the heart,
a reminder of the way
one soul lifts another
with the light it leaves
on a canvas,
in the pattern it weaves
with words,
in the way two souls
are twinned
in the purple dusk
of a moonlit night long ago,
remembered once more.

Spirits of Earth

Salmon and Water

When I came into this world, it was to be
with water. Born in the bed of a river,
I made my way to the ocean, my first love.

Before my body was done, I swam back
hundreds of miles against the current
to the serene stream of my birth
where I carved a bowl in its gravel,
gently laid the thousands I carried,
my shining orange pearls. Finally ready

to let go of the flesh of my body, I became
water, formed into ice, romanced a glacier,
and found love again.

Glacier and Monarch Butterfly

When the ice of our bodies could no longer
hold the warming, our layers slowly
melting into the sea, we transformed

into a kaleidoscope of migrating monarchs,
the transparent windows of our wings
reflecting the light of our love
across a continent, the curtain of our bodies
wrapped in treetops like a multitude
of stained-glass jewels lighting the dusk

until it was time to let our color fade and fall
to the forest floor where we became seeds
and rooted into a tree.

Tree and Eagle

When I was a sprout gathered with siblings
round the base of our mother, she nursed us
with her great roots. I drank the coastal fog,

let it soak into my soft, red skin, grew tall
like my kin, offered my branches and breath
for hundreds of years until the chisel of fire
hollowed my base and the mass
of my body fell into a bed of soft decay
that fed my hungry offspring. Letting go

of an earthbound life, the tips of my branches
became a wide span of wings flying high
above sunlit sapling faces.

Eagle and Man

When I soared over mountains and lakes,
dropped down to rivers and valleys,
glided wind currents for hours, rootless,

I grew hungry. My eyes knew how to eat,
able to see rabbits three miles away,
spot fish flitter beneath the water. I knew
the violence of a hunter, looked deeply
into the eyes of my prey, felt our bond,
began to see beyond myself. I folded

my tired wings in respect, closed the scope
of my strained eyes, fell into a dream,
awoke as man.

Man and Woman

When I was a man, most of our kind no longer
knew nature as relation, thought it was a threat
to conquer. In isolation, I grew afraid.

From fear, I took everything I could, took
more, felt it as power, thought it was love,
learned too late it was not. I left it all behind
with the bones of my body as my tears
turned into a woman whose heart had been
broken so many times it began to open.

When I became a woman, I loved the curves
of my body like the hills and hollows of home.
As it aged, I cherished my furrowed skin and
slow gait that gave me time. I rejoiced the loss
of desire to cling to who I believed I should be,
let go of useless ideologies. When I finally fell

back into the earth like all the others, spirit
became formless, resting between earth and sky,
waiting for love to become again.

Not Alone

When the path narrows
and the way forward
darkens like the deep
center of a forest
as tall shadows
of unfamiliar trees
close in
from all directions
and there is no choice
but to merge
with the blackness,

it is then we see a lone
glow in the distance,
a barely perceptible
shimmer beckoning
as if to tell us
even in darkness
we are not alone,
to remind us we are held
with all the others
waiting
for the light to find us.

The Guide That Comes in Darkness

A soul-stopping sound pierced through
our dream-laden sleep, a heart-rattling cry
in the hour of darkness when nothing

seems solid. As it came closer, its long wail
reverberated against the walls of our bodies,
and pierced our ears with a pitch we could not
bear. It was not a species we could name,

our categories were useless, failed comforts.
Without words to guide us, we grew afraid
in this new place, decades and landscapes
from where we once called home. Native

to nowhere now, we had no feel for fauna
here – though even a native would be lost
to this sound. Unable to construct meaning,
our way of thinking undone, we could only

feel. We felt its primal force, feared it was
merciless like Grendel unleashed, or lost
and alone, crying out for its mother
or its mother's cry, inconsolable like death.

The guide that comes in darkness comes first
as fear and offers only the unrecognizable,
like the black marsh beyond our backyard
inhabited by the unknown or unknowable.

In our quiet trembling, we did not cry out
like ancient warriors who knew their enemies
and their gods. We were alone at the shadow's
edge with our own private monster or savior,

we knew not which. Grown weary of our fear,
we found solace in surrender. Without words,
we heard the sacred silence within us. Now,
we watch over the sound, and it is our guide.

What Is Bridged

~ reflection on Claude Monet's water garden at Giverny

What is bridged in the crossing
over the slight arch of wooden slats
hewn into a garden bridge –
its beginning and end hidden
in the lush mystery of willows?

What arises in watchers as they lean
over deep-green rails, drawn in
by the pond's pull, its dream-like
impressions reflecting another time
beneath the shade of a pergola
where wistful wisteria hang down
into their longing to touch the surface
where water lilies lift up like magic
from the fertile secrets of mud?

What dreams or impressions persist,
what longings or secrets stay
with those who pause, mirrored
in a bridge of time as they cross over?

Nest of Creation

~ inspired by *The Domain of Arnheim* painting by Rene Magritte

God is a great gray bird
opening her wide wingspan
of mountain peaks
powdered with freshly fallen
snow layered over feathers
of ancient blue glaciers
as the twilight
of a sliver moon perches above
her infinite watchfulness
and illuminates the bright
white jewels held
in her nest of creation.

A Deeper View

Are we not vessels after all
holding a life shaped by years
into the form we needed to be
as we expanded out
to hold the lives of others?

Did we not learn to round
our edges and heal
from within as we narrowed
back into our own life
as we must do in the end?

And did we not break through
this earthen sphere
into the light we saw beyond
and join the confluence
of the ten directions to shape
the future with a deeper view?

ABOUT THE AUTHOR

Chera Van Falcon Burg grew up in Rochester, New York near Lake Ontario with her parents, older brother and four younger siblings. Their family home was surrounded by parkland, which was the ancestral lands of the Seneca. The park with its creek, marshlands, meadows, hills, woods, birds and wildlife provided a childhood refuge from a difficult family life and instilled a deep sense of the natural world and its healing essence.

Chera began writing poetry at a young age in response to her experience in nature. She won a county-wide poetry contest when she was ten years old and her poem was published in the Rochester newspaper. As an undergraduate, she minored in both philosophy and writing, and has participated in numerous poetry classes and workshops since then. Her poems have been published in poetry journals, newspapers, CD jackets and poetry trails. She has performed her poetry with musicians in venues and festivals in the US, Mexico, and Europe.

Chera is an award-winning filmmaker and environmental activist. She co-wrote and produced the film, *Call Of Life*, about the drivers of the current mass extinction crisis and its cultural and psychological underpinnings. The film won The Best Science Communication Film Award at the Reel Earth Environmental Film Festival in New Zealand, the Earth Vision Jury Award at the Santa Cruz Film Festival, a Finalist Award at the International Wildlife Film Festival, and the John Muir Gold Award at the Yosemite Film Festival. As producer of the film, Chera was awarded the Accolade Humanitarian Award by the Accolade Global Film Competition.

In her teens, Chera took an interest in eastern philosophy and states of consciousness, including meditation and dreams, which led to her to study psychology, including the work of Carl Jung. She moved to the San Francisco Bay Area to complete her doctorate in psychology and was fortunate to train with renowned existential and humanistic psychologist, Rollo May. As a psychologist, Chera published in psychology journals, was a professor of psychology in California and New York, had a private practice, and was a senior psychologist/supervisor at San Quentin State Prison where she developed and directed a psychology doctoral internship program.

As a climate migrant from the smoke and wildfires of California, Chera eventually moved to Door County, Wisconsin in 2022 where she participates in three monthly poetry critique groups with former and current county poet laureates. She writes poetry to navigate the mystery of being alive on this planet as part of the natural world in relationship with all other beings here.